# Noah's Arkestra



Daemon Dewing

BookLeaf Publishing

Presentation by *BookLeaf Publishing*

Web: www.bookleafpub.com

E-mail: info@bookleafpub.com

ISBN: 9789357440578

First edition 2023

# DEDICATION

Dedicated to my parents, wise and loving, who sacrificed much more than a son can ever appreciate and never lost faith through thick and thin. To my wife Rowena, who is unfailingly loyal and suffers my idiosyncrasies with grace and the unshakable calm of her Anglo-Indian heritage. To my children Zara and Eva, who must be inspired to be the best people they can be. Finally, to my Sufi master Dr Javad Nurbakhsh, who in emptying his cloak, bequeathed a legacy of loving kindness to his Murids, in a world much at odds with itself.

# PREFACE

The author had the great fortune to meet many remarkable people from the North Caucasian society of Chechnya, victims of brutal conflicts from the 1990s. The author was attracted by the commonality of Sufism and drawn in by the Russian-speaking milieu with its own rich literary tradition  He found the opportunity to experience remarkable moments of humanity which have graced his life in innumerable ways. Working with refugees over 20 years has led to lifelong friendships that feel more than just worldly attachments and reflect deep mysterious ties that only the creator can know the reason for.

# A Definition Of Poetry

It is the soft sound of a blown kiss,
Fluttering like the lone moth,
through the ravenous dark night,
To a lonely outpost of light.
On the edge of beyond,
Holding off dark legions till dawn.
It is wine sweetened with tears of joy,
Bread leavened by pain,
sacred communion in bloodied rain.
It is the kiss of blood-red lips,
On the white robes of purity.
It is a night lit up by hope,
when fear spars with the nightingale.
It is the blow of the axe,
Slicing the air into precise halves.
It is the universe's chime,
Shimmering in eternal stasis,
Wrapped up in verse,
Encoded in scripts within codes.
It's the stanzas of falling rain,
On the couplets of fertile imagination.
Its words sprouting into verse,
From chaos- meaning!
Transmuting hard hearts of stone,
Strange symbols infiltrate the language
Of the heart,

Striking where no arrow can.
Its stars fallen from the sky like swans,
gliding on the moonlit pond
Just out of reach of outstretched arms.
It is the heavenly abode falling to earth,
The worship of roses,
To the sky god.
But most of all,
It is you and I.

# For A Fistful Of Earth

I am tired of empty faces,
Of vacuous eyes, hollowed out like
The glaze of winter's dawn.
Carry me away to the Sultan's palace
On the wings of the firebird!
Let my ashes be scattered in with his,
In the bountiful resurrection.
The spark from the eye
Of love's knowledge,
ignites the heart in a fireball of desire!
See them with their leaden feet,
Shackled by attachment to this
Fleeting world.
See how willingly they dig their graves!
lined by property and possessions,
like falsehoods and rancor
cast on a pyre of vanity!
I will not live in their icy cold shadows
Where there is no shelter nor warmth,
like in a miraged desert frozen at night,
day scorched minds find no respite.
I have overheard words prattled,
by the holy and profane,
by those who professed religion,
but had not a shred of soul.

Like birds at a frenzied conference,
No wisdom, but the idle
chatter of empty shells.
mistook for sacred divination,
Hollow rings of an emptying eternity
Long overdue to those who have
Outstayed their welcome,
In this world which puts the spirit to form
To see with his eyes,
But envision with his love.
and like Gods to
rise from the relative to the absolute.
Pity those then who burnt down heaven
For a few fistfuls of earth.

# The Bosom Bereft

In the cleft of the bosom bereft,
Lies a sorrow in shards once the shape of a
child,
Like a darkening space,
Imploded by light turning in on itself.
Heaving breath churns out a tempest of rage.
Befuddled and muddled emotions swirl like
Fighting cocks in a storm of feathered fury.
The heart's sinews tear at what could have been,
Time and again the mind plays over and over
The same frozen slow-motion picture
Of a pain that sits in still motion,
fractionated in shattered slivers,
Each a private slip of agony.
Anger and sorrow howl across an
Inky black lake of no return,
Like dark wolves in a moon-bathed night,
Smoky offspring, in marbled twilight!
A shivering sorrow heats itself
by angers fiery glow,
but cannot warm itself,
colder still
With chattering teeth and teared eyes.
Hands tremble,
fingers supplicate to a God that failed,

a prayer cloaked in nonbelief,
like the sun swallowed
by the inky black void.
Rhythmic, mesmeric, trancelike transcendent
sorrow.
A coffin passes, like flotsam on the sea
Bobbing and rising and falling with the tide of
Breathed out tears.
A murmur from the crowd, and a tight stabbing
pain
So cold one feels Decembered in two.
Her last non-meeting with her spring child,
The last burnt-up splendid day,
Gone.
Forever is too final,
And her blood is too clotted to fill
The cup of life any longer,
With anything but sorrow's bittering
dregs.

# Burn The Ships

When the sea blows up an unholy storm,
when my sails are sodden and torn,
When my crew is beyond mutinies rules
On this sinking ship of holy fools
When the eye of the storm casts its furious gaze,
Over our worst hopes and fears raised,
When the bottom of the ocean is nearer than
land
And despair has taken our anchor in hand
Dragging down to the dark depths raging
Far beyond the plumb lines gauging
When there is no hope and the dove of peace
Exhaustedly plunged into the dark waters
beneath
It's time to burn the ships,
Dry your tears men and step into a new day!
Light the last match,
and burn the ships by your own hand,
And take the eternal land!
These ghost ships floating on seas of nowhere,
Like floating graves for
Men not dead yet not living,
Are no place for the pilgrim soul, striving
across endless oceans spanned,
Seeking out that Holy Land.

So dive into the world's raging swell,
Knowing heaven's path is crossed by hell's.
Scuttle your desires against the riptide,
Give in to his swirling currents and ride,
Swimming through seas of shame and sorrow,
And fight to see the sun-drenched morrow,
Be like flotsam and jetsam of a wreck,
After the storm on gentled sea bedecked,
Be a wreckage of hope and joys.
Faith and love are your life-marking buoys.
In the mad moments of that tempest's roar,
That guides you steadily to the eternal shore,
With its endless horizon of skies of gold.
So burn the ships,
and in the wreckage of your soul,
take the Holy Land of old.

# Every Shard

The ground glass tide of time,
Cracking in fractionated ecstasy,
Shimmering slivered mirrors,
Of being, and non-being, make
A quantum kaleidoscopic riot of possibility.
Washes up as probability,
in the circus of the absurd.
The dark shadow of none being,
The throbbing abyss of endless possibilities,
pulsates at the event horizon of light.
The moment of reality is born at the edge of
Madness!
The footfall into oblivion, frozen in a
Moment of realisation.
Here and now, back and beyond.
Light and dark.
All opposites united in the singular moment of
now,
The fall into divine madness, is the ascent into
eternal majesty.
Endless dark, eternal light.
I am each and every shard,
Lived out in infinite being and non-being,
The quantum of here and there and not
anywhere

yet everywhere.
Like a bow I stretch in being, my string pulled
Taut in equal and opposite way,
Like my soul bridged by irreconcilable opposites
Held together by Non-being.
the silent spaces between the arc of my soul.
I shoot at life itself. existence collapses into the
Quivering ripple of my bowstring.
My arrow passes through being and non-being
Bound for the domain of no return.
A transient fireball in the canvas of night,
Writes its story across the starlit sky.
In a fiery script burning itself out,
Across the page of here and now,
and is then gone forever
as if it never were

# In The Shadow Of The Cross

You kissed me in the shadow of the cross,
As a heartbeat cried across the blood red sky,
Like a white shroud, dragged along a reddened
path.
Soaking anguish and pain into a
Bloodied prayer mat of martyrdom.
Forgiveness opened the door to eternal life.
As death was closing the earthly chapter,
On a book short read.
You grasped the thorn of crowns,
Your bloody coronation,
took up love's duties uncomplaining
on your bloodied head, as you
carried a cross of other's woes on the road
To Calvary.
These footsteps, crossed many times before,
By lovers who sowed a speck of heavenly hope,
And reaped a whirlwind of worldly woes.
Yet our love is unending strength,
like the beam on which we nail our
Sacrifice of this temporal world for the realm
eternal.
Like an Astrolabe that guides,
The celestial soul encased in clay.

Carrying the weight of man's sin as lightly as a bird
Carries its feathers.
We soar the heavens on the wings of love,
Even as our carnal state mires us in clay.
God is unending unfathomable love,
Depths with no end and beginning,
Consumes in an instant those who surrender
Their ear to the call of the heart.
The prince of thieves will steal your heart
With his song to sweet surrender.
Love is the reward, its beginning and its end.
Forgive them then, for they know not what they do.
It is done.

# The Maths Of Life

You are obsessed with the maths of life,
I live for the algebra of the moment
Where 'X' marks the spot.
You seek to contain, maintain and quantify,
I seek to unravel, travel and become.
You are disparate, divided and relative.
I am everywhere and nowhere at once,
Living in the moment, I live on
The sharp edge of eternity,
Abstracted to the back of beyond,
Way beyond the darkened limits of knowledge's
Barren wastelands.
In your every fibre, my song breathes
Life into your atomic reasoning.
I am an absolute being.
You pour wine into a cup and ask how much?
I say what cup, what wine?
I am the drink of the drink,
beyond spirits spirit even!
My intoxication is the wine's essence.
My place of knowing union.
No place in the world of cold reason,
For this Shangri La of the heart.
Fools calculate the heat of my love in endless
Fahrenheits, yet freeze

In the mono season of endless winter.
The maniacal machine mind
Of heartless measures, losses and gain.
Unable to die,
For it has never lived.
Trapped in an eternal loop of
Smoke and mirrors,
Prattling into oblivion,
Victim of the Matrix.
But I live on unchanging,
The King of Zeroes.
For I reside at the interchange of the cross,
Decimalised between life and death,
Being and none being,
Riding the atomic scales
Balanced to the last atom.
I never was, and never will be,
I simply am X.
The master equation you will never solve.

# The Golden River

The beguiling call of posthumous glory,
Like a siren bestride a rocky outcrop,
Calling sailors bold and reckless
To a watery grave.
The call enters my ears, but settles on my soul.
To turn the vague feeling of life,
Into a tangible measure of being?
Can only be paid by the ultimate price.
What is the sentence but naught
Without the full stop?
The living mostly, as blood and mud
Baked into equal parts.
come as they go,
from ashes to ashes,
dust to dust.
But those who for love,
Through love,
And by love,
separated spirit from frame,
Have settled for immortalised name.
Ever young in the glorious flush,
Of youth that knows no autumnal fall,
Nor winter's funeral shroud that hangs
On the living.
They have exchanged the relative form,

like droplets returning to
the ocean of glory.
How I envy those who looked Charon in the eye,
And passing over,
Spat out their coin,
Tumbling into
His emaciated fingers,
the cold bony grip
stretched across all time.
The rite of passage defied.
Sunk traceless into the river Styx Charon
and this price
Well paid.
The inky waters in an instant
turned golden
Immortal.
Cerberus bowed his head thrice at the triple
Crown of courage of those,
Living to die to live forever.

# Winter Reigns

Then the rains began, the day the clowns left town,
The big top collapsed down like a billowing chador.
The red-faced juggler, the square-jawed muscle man,
Where are they now the rains are under endless grey skies?
Laughter and summer interred under a darkened frown.
A smiling poster looked out of season,
Fluttering ragged in autumn's wintery scowl.
A gathering storm of pictures and posters congregated,
Bereft of joy, precisely hopeless, a slow steady
Dance into a swirling mass on an empty desolate street,
Squaring up to fight out the grey day away.
We had trailed their dreams watching their routines,
With mouths open wide,
As daredevils' tormented death high in the air,
With somersaults that laughed at despair.
Pensive, in a sadness of passing life
They urged us to seize the moment,

To live in that instant that is shorter
Than the blink of an eye, yet longer
than all eternity.
And what now, of these empty streets?
That pristine field where life overflowed
In ecstatic joy,
is now a cloying swamp of rain and mud.
The coming storm, over the brow of frowning
mountains,
presages winter's cold-blooded kiss.
Hurling migrant birds across chilly skies
Come the legions of winter.
Wind, rain and the shroud of snow,
To bury all sign there ever was life,
That for one magical moment,
made time stand still.

# The Science Of Goodbyes

With precise vagueness, overflows emptiness
From my unhearted chest,
A sunken treasure from depths where
A titanic heartsink rests,
sparkles in the blackened shade,
Of the parting of decembered friends.
Bittersweet the parting,
Sorrow offered itself in dowry
for a wedding that never could be.
My reddened eyes struggle under a burden
Of wept sodden tears dried like,
hewn rocks from a salt mine of sadness.
I saw the Acropolis in flames, across a
millennial arc,
As if time had smeared, like paint across a
canvas,
a love-struck artist's elegy
All of time like a continuum,
I saw the flames snuffed out in a spark.
I saw your face fall into history's arms,
And I loved you the more for your distance.
Aeons have kept us apart,
But our love is bejewelled by a robe of stars,
Sparkling across the belly of all time,
Ever bright, ever constant, guided by
The astrolabe of his name.

The multiverse hums its eternal chant,
Every moment of time living in perfect unison,
Outside of time and place and person.
The quantum strikes even as it parts,
Casting realities into fragments of absolute being.
Each shard parting from the source.
You come and go and come again,
I go, and I stay gone.
This is the precise meaning of goodbye.

# Under The Oak Tree

Under the Oak Tree
What does a man think of under the oak tree?
Leaves rustling above at ease, in an air that
breathes
its own hot breath,
a vapour one day,
a hoary frost the next.
And seasons come and seasons go.
In the blink of an eye, the boy turns to man.
What does a man think of under the oak tree?
As he locks his loved ones into caskets of oak,
His memories,
Her silken thread of life to death.
Looking into the eyes of the living,
Touched by their memories,
His imprinted heart
Partakes of the simple joys,
Then lies down to a great sleep.
A childhood fly,
Straight out of the magical yesterday
alights on his hand,
Quivering like the atoms of his being,
Two eyes stare at a multitude,
The fly washes carefully, oblivious
So he plucks at the wings of an imagined time,

He recollects the oak tree from which
He espied land far on the clouded horizon,
Perched precariously up a dizzying mast
of childhood's long sailed ship.
Months at sea his childish reverie,
Pass in an instant.
The fly sits cleaning itself
oblivious,
And pirates battle with buccaneers,
Cutlasses swinging at an air
Heavy with timelessness.
He moves,
The fly with him too, rolling on the sea
Of dreams, that floods around him.
Sweet drownings in the magic
of childhood memories,
Where stones grumble as they are kicked across
the path,
Where every path in gloaming glades is entry
To other worlds,
The joy of infinite possibilities.
He is happy this hairy insect moves up his arm,
Sampling every moment of his childhood.
I want to smash my watch,
To freeze time in that moment
Of great delight,
Under the oak tree.
The fly, oblivious, buzzes once,
And in an instant, is gone.

# Unlearning

When was it that realisation came,
Mother and father were children themselves
of the same holy father?
When came the moment when mortality stepped
Out into the realm of eternity?
And cast down the garments of knowing
For a shimmering robe of freedom?
How I had to unlearn in the highest degree
truths nature!
My illusions had to be shattered,
in this glass trinket world.
So life and death could no longer cast
different shadows.
And time collapsed in a heap like a cloak
emptied of its Sage.
I see life in shimmering frequencies now,
In and out of time,
All moments of time alive in
An eternal moment,
With no past or present.
Sometimes a Roman's nose or a
Turkoman's gaze.
Men of grim iron,
Idol worshippers.
Another time a Khan's inscrutable eyes,

And sometimes I spy a fearful future
with old sorrows baked from the same
old clay pot.
the base smell of which drives up my nostrils
flying straight into my mind's eye.
I see a family struggling on the edge of life,
Thin-bellied children like emaciated gazelles,
Grubby and wretched,
All of mankind waiting on the few,
And how they survived, and how they thrived
When all had almost been close to nought.
And then I think I spy reality,
like a sun, beaming so many rays
all from one point of truth.
This universe compacted to a speck on a pinhead
of divine glory!
And I am sun blinded in this
Starburst of knowing.
There is no knowledge and no ignorance,
No right and no wrong
In the universal law.
All is one, an undivided whole.
All is unity by its very being.
And I am at peace with myself.
The Buddha knew better than to speak,
For in truth
These truths have no words.

# When You Are No More

When others talk,
It's only your words I hear.
It's their tongues but it's your script in your play
Where you are the only actor.
When laughter erupts,
It's your tear-filled eyes I see reflecting back,
Irony, truth and mockery
In a dewy teardrop
Deeper than the ocean.
You laugh at your own cosmic joke
idiotic and holy at once.
It's you sitting on that train carriage
Your hair just obscuring your radiant face.
At the table I see
The half-drunk tea is yours alone,
You are cup, dregs and their divined future
All at once.
The jangle of bracelets I hear in the
Street are our wedding bands,
Binding us to the cupbearer,
Who pours forth water to wine again.
The sweet serving girl,
Her smile is yours, her frown yours alone,
The heaving bosom and delicate waist
All is yours.

When they are all gone,
it's as if they never were,
Yet you alone are most real
when you are not.

# The Word

The world was born from the silence of word unspoke,
Sitting in nonexistence, basking in the imaginal realm,
Legions of possibilities clashing arms,
Cutting down what could have been,
Until the victor of what was to be took form.
First the hapless planktons of lower being,
Forebears of life on earth's unseen realms.
Taking forms beyond the eye of faith or reason,
Unfathomable depths of existence, form
Within form within form.
And so the creator began to speak,
And matter massed ranks,
To abide by the command to live.
And life began its journey from the empty
Outer reach, slowly
Painfully, casting off form with ruthless strokes
Of evolutions blade, paring down all that should not be.
First brutes ruled the earth,
Their reign ending in the rain of terror
As light left the skies bereft,
Choking all beneath its heated gaze.

And then strange beings that ancient tongues
Once spoke of,
From the temptation of an apple,
Rotten to the core but sacred in form,
Rose upon its two feet.
That cursed race of man…
Soon the village drum beat became the drum roll of war,
Families estranged by aeons and continents,
At one another's throats,
Ancient feuds placed brother against brother.
Now today the lost tribes of man
Find their way back to the family hearth.
Back to the word,
Silent, unspeakable, illimitable.
In unity is the sacred word made song,
The song of love that makes
All things possible.

# Frogs In The Well

If my mouth wounds with words ills spoke,
Do not think of me so unwell,
But treat me lightly like a madman whose
Tongue untied ran loose
Down a labyrinth of endless horizons.
So look at the hapless frogs in their well!
Who from exile of well- narrow views
preposterous proportions spies,
False horizons on falsely spied skies.
How much ideology can a frog swallow
Spouting from his tiny well, the ideas
Of a world that has no place for the heart,
But with ordered rules and regulations,
turns a man inhuman.
I smashed my rosary in disgust
When I heard there was no place for love
On this endless road.
I tore up my prayer mat in despair
That this God has no heart,
No mercy to forgive the transgressor's step.
Why does brother's blood spill on the floor,
When you can see our familial traits?
The smile on a face is divine,
How can you smash your brother's face
To tears of blood because he sees

God's face in his loved one's eyes?
The divine is here and there,
Immanent and permanent.
He resides in every atom of our being,
In the love, laughter and smiles of
Our friends.
Why do you confine him to books?
Bind him with the chains of dogma and
ideology?
His jailers are Priests and Mullahs.
You have beat and battered him wherever
You saw him stir in a man's heart
And turned the temples to Mausolea.
This is not the house of God,
But a graveyard.
His life is the smile of my friends,
The laughter of my child.
In the blood I will shed to protect his love.
But still you croak of rules!
For a cosied view from a well,
you have denied the ocean of being.

# Tyranny

Tyranny always seeks to justify itself,
Bringer of law and order to chaos,
governor of those who are ungovernable.
Friend of power, enemy of freedom,
The tyrant's vision always through
The iron fist.
No bitter pill of consensus,
No bowing to the authority of learned men,
Nor wisdom receiver,
For tyranny is wisdom and authority in one,
All-knowing, unquestionable,
Fanned by a coterie of liars and flatterers,
Featherers whose own fragile nests lie
In the lion's mane,
Fear the roar of he pricked by
The thorn of democracy.
So the wound festers,
And as all is stable,
the rot sets deeper inside,
Biding its time for when the statues shall fall
And scrap merchants shall feast.
His legacy? the torture chambers of medieval
Inquisition,
for sedition must be torn
Limb from limb.

And the hushed whispers of people
Who for years will not dare
Mention his name…
And his epitaph the graves
Of those he buried for daring
to clutch at another vision.
But, like the day of judgement,
the corpses shall rise en masse
demanding justice,
For never at rest,
the dead animate the living.

# The Cradle Of Humanity

Deep in Medea's mist-shrouded mountains,
Lie treasures exceeding madmen’s spoutings.
Dark craggy cliffs, like silent sentinels do
resolutely hold
A priceless beating heart of pure molten gold,
Locked deep in Mount Kaf’s heavy breast,
God's earthly hidden treasure chest.
Towering in snow-capped silent splendour,
This guard of honour with peaks like bayonets to
render
the bravest hearts in two.
Deep at the mighty feet of Elbruz and Ararat,
Lies man’s delicate cradle, rocking in the
Winds of immemorial harakat.
White peaks tear heaven’s roof asunder,
Ensheathed in legend and crowned by thunder.
No human sound breaks the awful silence of
these giants.
Their heads caught the stars as Zeus fought with
Typhoeus,
As Frost Giants struggled with Odin for eternal
glory,
Stars fell like sparks from the blacksmith’s anvil,
Fired by the sacred flame, a smelter of men!
Prometheus caught hold of the spark,

Clutching at his immolated immortality,
He endured unending agony as chained to
A stone table of desire, liver was rent from his
shuddering frame on a living funeral pyre.
This boundary of the world so far from freedom
swallowed his roars without a soul to hear,
The awesome silence even mighty Zeus did
quiver in fear.
Next came man in a second coming,
Like flotsam and jetsam of an unholy flood,
The Ark of the covenant spared man's filial
blood
Suckled on Ararat's two mighty breasts.
Noah's children survived, then thrived, in this
new garden of Eden, by God's decree.
Till cruel King Amiran, raised wickedness
To legendary degree.
Then the people wept and plead,
That they might be freed from tyrannies dread.
The master of the world, heard his evil cackle,
And cast the wicked king, in mighty shackles,
deep into Ararat's labyrinthine chest.
With only a savage hound for his companion.
Canine loyalty knows no evil, but loves for
love's sake,
So by constant gnawing did hound with
slavering jaw
The chains nearly breeching,
at the evil master's beseeching.

Cavernous and dank his gaping maw.
Thus mighty anvils must clank not once, not twice
But on new year's eve but thrice,
To reinforce freedom's reign,
by repairing once again, evil Amiran's chain.
Crowning Ararat's lofty ice-crowned crest,
the Simurg, King of birds, doth make his nest.
With one eye piercing the past known and unread,
another eye divines the future far ahead.
His rule over kingdom's invisible beyond unseen,
Where Djinnistan, only manifests, to hearts pure clean.
He knows all of the heroes, the future will need,
and summons each a Djinn, their soul to feed.
Rumbling in Elbruz's bowels, awaiting the spark
Gog and Magog wait in underworld dark,
ready for that final day of reckoning.
When the Lord shall summon by celestial beckoning,
the end of days of righteous men,
when chaos shall rule and swords bloody the dawn.
Blood in a trickle, then a flood, and Elburz shall mourn,
And wickedness shall goodness sweep
From the face of the earth that shall weep,

as love is swept away from home's hearth.
And only tear-stained eyes of ochre rivers,
Shall evidence of Elbruz's fatherly love,
He failed to deliver.
As the cradle he rocked from high above,
is burnt black to the ground,
Where ashes and earth are together pound.
Where man's passing cannot be found,
Where no trace of man may be rallied,
But a whispered verse, in strange tongue,
shall haunt forgotten valleys,
Passing through darkened woods,
And fall  howling on the open plain,
Some call it the song of Ragnarok's reign.

# The Devil's gold

In vain you cast treasures at my feet,
greatness, fame and limitless power,
Won't defeat
the passion of my poetry,
To drown my seekers' tears with gold.
You tried offering diamonds to outsparkle,
the tears of my joyous road,
when the sun rises, and my tears,
like crystal droplets, water the dewy morn
with love, at this sheer joy of being born.
Yet still death hovers at my doors hearth,
a wraith of a long darkening path,
into the hazy beyond.
his eyes, an inky black void, pour
from the great nothing, that stretches
beyond stanzas, that like signposts
or rotten teeth fall away over

the stretched canvas of decades.
A hundred times I lay in the grave, waiting
like Lazarus for a cold rebirth.
My poems like incantations to the
God of the dead, crossed the worlds.
Ghosts delighted in my couplets
living once again between the
heavy space of my stanzas, which
breathed life into the cold recesses
of death's chilling breath.
And the devil seeing this,
could not bear, that the veil might rent
twixt the worlds.
So he came at me with his horns
and claws, thrusting gold before me,
such promises, such delights
for the silence of my art.
That the page might stay blank and
no words escape into the there beyond.
that the veil might remain unbreached.
And when reasoning and bribes would
not undo the poet's tongue,
a full storming rage! as legions
of his vile hordes howled at night
rattling my shutters.
They bayed for my blood,
so I gave it full writ,
on the parchment of my own skin.
written in glistening blood,

that for all time there is no here nor there,
that death is but an illusion.
that each and every deed small and great,
each and every thought,
whether filled by love or hate,
exists for all time,
not ceased by a veil of mortal fate.
As we are here and now,
we shall always be, immortal beings.

# Little Birdsong

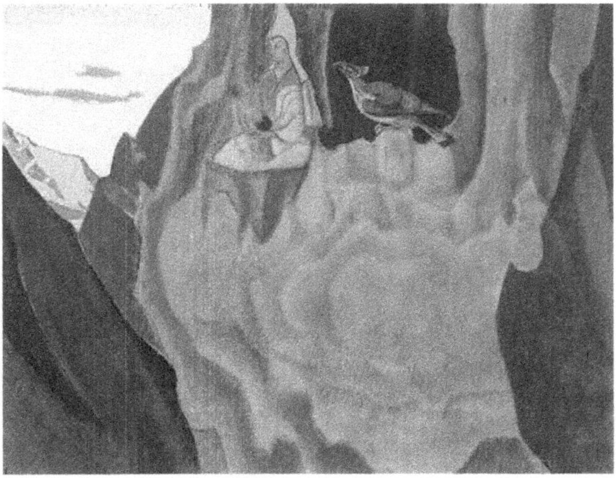

The cold December air stabs at my shrunken ribs,
But nothing touches that little bird of hope,
Who on the bower of despair sings freedom's song.
This gallant troubadour rallies routed heart and soul.
A chill wind had settled on my heart in the cold
Long night of my soul.
Blown away hope, frozen my will to carry on.
Freedom was a distant memory,
The pristine expanses of my childhood range,
Hacked down to the dimensions of this monastic cell.

But though bars on the window kept me within,
The song passed through from without.
Lit up my heart with hope, in this world of
lament.
For this is the song my father heard too, in his
exile,
that sustained him through dark valleys
of the long nights of the soul.
So he might gather sinew and soul anew, to face
down
Oppressions glare.
Long lost his childhood lands, never again to set
eyes upon.
Yet his head never bowed to oppressions'
demand,
His eye unflinchingly met the enslavers' stare.
They tried to brutalise him as one might master a
beast but
Though body ached and bled from tyranny's
whip,
He kept the soul song alive, nurtured by an
unbending faith,
Faith thicker than any cell door, surer than any
chain.
And now in darkest night, when he is buried so
deep and so long gone,
Does he return to me on the wings of this song.
That hope must eternally fight with despair.

Must unfailingly smile through all blows and declare,
That love conquers all, enslaves all the more surely,
than walls of bricks and clay, can close in captivities gaze.
That love's enslavement of the heart,
is the beginning of the golden dawn of day,
of freedom's march away from this world of transient pain.
Love transports in a moment freed men to joyous captivity,
and slaves to freedom's boundless plain.
The bestowal of love's grace, unites opposing parts,
In an instant jailer and jailed have no door to
Separate their one heart.
And freedom an attitude of the soul,
Screams out in ecstasy overwhelmed at its
Birth pangs into this eternal world.
No longer bitter the whips crack,
More like the flail of devotion.
And the prison walls have been torn down,
The gloom of winter's grey canvas torn asunder,
Pours through blinding light in an explosion of thunder.
Manacles that tied me down, now raise me up,
For I am my father's son.
Eternal, indestructible, as eternal

As time itself.
The song of freedom has brought spring to my heart,
In the deepest winter of my mind.
Manacles may shackle my earthly frame, but my heart is as
Free as a bird on the wing-
Wings of love that carry me on winds of everlasting joy.

# I am the Spark

I am that spark that sets alight, the love of your
heart,
I am the glance that pierces your defence's from
the dark charms, of one enshrouded, in
black-eyed mystery.
I play havoc with your tears wringing
bittersweet wine
From your birth pangs cries.
Drink deep my friend!
You have fallen out of favor, yet my merest
stirrings
salve your sinner's soul, with a drop from
my cup of eternal grace and favor.
You, who are imaginer and imagined, cannot
grasp the
Boundless horizons of my love that permeate
your every pore!
I have sculpted mountains, cast seas into a
cascade of
frenzied foam and tide.
I besequinned the skies with twinkling fireballs,
My celestial joke of a billion suns.
You cannot endure the heat of my love, so like
stars placed light years beyond

I allow you a temporal look of eternal joy,
You glimpse my sacred tapestry in nights of longing,
Before I fold up the night sky and push you into a brave new dawn.
You think you are ruled by time and space,
That your being is relative to all in the physical realm,
But I tell you, you are the alpha and the omega,
You are the trillions of atoms that whirr you into this illusion,
the dance of everlasting joy!
The realm of infinite possibility, screams a multitude of existences,
out of your every pore and fibre.
Living your life turns your eye to form and deceit,
but true consciousness burns all illusion before it, on a pyre
Of a gnostic brilliant blinding light.
You cannot not be, cannot fall out of existence into none being.
You are all that is and ever has been.
Eternal without beginning and end...
Said the beloved in response:
You who are the word of the word, the heart of the heart,
I was slain under the triumphal arches of your celestial brow,

when you raised them to me, and raised me to immortality!
I have loved you so fiercely from such deep depths of this cup,
that the dregs have caught in my throat like poison-tipped arrows
from a hunter's arched bow.
As I drink hard of this impassioned love,
I drown in a sea of love battered by waves of ecstasy!
Eternal is the love of the heart,
The only reality in this world of passing forms,
a world of sorrow and crazy joy!
You who are my astrolabe, my journey and my destiny.

# The Duel Of The Poets

The poets faced off in a duel of verse refined,
A fight to the death with words and lines.
Metred verse like dragooned massed ranks,
Where loss for words was victory sank.
Stanzas glistening like polished swords
Bloodied bayonets of the golden horde.
Passionate will to live, yet glad to die,
Tight verse, forward ho! they let the poetry fly.
A firestorm of verse in a fusillade of shattering shot,
Screams of pain, the heat of battle fiery hot.
Verses scythed listeners with hearts torn to sorrow
At the darkened moment of the reaper's morrow.
Hopes held high cast down to the funeral pyre,
scattered battlefield words, kindled the smoked bier.
from the earth back to mud,
Word for word, blood for blood.
The oath by which these verse warriors bind,
To live and die by the words they find.
To express lives in fidelity lived true,
To reveal by word the hearts every hue.
So bold these exalted Bards,
Hearts pricked by love's barbed shards.
The seasoned warrior in his inflamed heart
His life balanced on the blade point of art!

He invoked one sacred Ramadan night,
Angelic miracles, to shine forth bright,
And illuminate the voice of his heart,
To make divine the clay tongue's art!
This night of Kadir falls but once each year,
Protector of poets, to his true lovers it's clear,
The Archangel raises up to dizzying stature,
the bard whose heart overflows with rapture,
With God's zealous love like wine spilling from
cup!
The poet's words-  like spears he hurls,
his love-struck stanzas, like victory standard
unfurls
On the battlefield of words where they
retort and repost line by line.
Till poetic metred ranks do his opponent unbind.
Grim-faced the Bard finishes with coup de
grace,
Turning to the judges for approval's face,
The learned wise men their heads held tight,
Turn to the victor, 'time to extinguish the light!'
From the stricken opponent on the floor laid low,
His head removed with single metered blow.
The champion of verse and song,
holds aloft the bloodied head to the throng.
"Here behold a noble knight, who lived by his
code,
whose life pure spoke, sang only of the eternal
ode.

www.ingramcontent.com/pod-product-compliance
Lightning Source LLC
Chambersburg PA
CBHW051737130826
49812CB00033B/901
*9789357440578*